HAL LEONARD STUDENT PIANO LIBRARY

INTERMEDIATE

Piano Recital Showcase

DUET FAVORITES

5 ORIGINAL DUETS FOR 1 PIANO/4 HANDS

CONTENTS

ISBN 978-1-4584-2243-9

HAL•LEONARD®
CORPORATION
7777 W. BLUEMOUND RD. P.O. BOX 13819 MILWAUKEE, WI 53213

In Australia Contact:
Hal Leonard Australia Pty. Ltd.
4 Lentara Court
Cheltenham, Victoria, 3192 Australia
Email: ausadmin@halleonard.com.au

Visit Hal Leonard Online at
www.halleonard.com

Angel Falls

for Gordon, my Angel

From a high plateau, majestically rising from the dense jungles of Venezuela,
cascades the incomparable Angel Falls. Nearly impossible to be approached except by helicopter,
Angel Falls is the highest waterfall in the world, with a drop of 3,212 feet.

By Sondra Clark

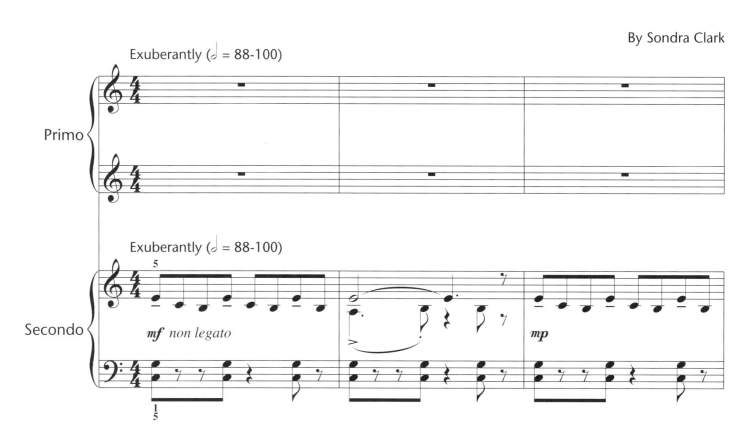

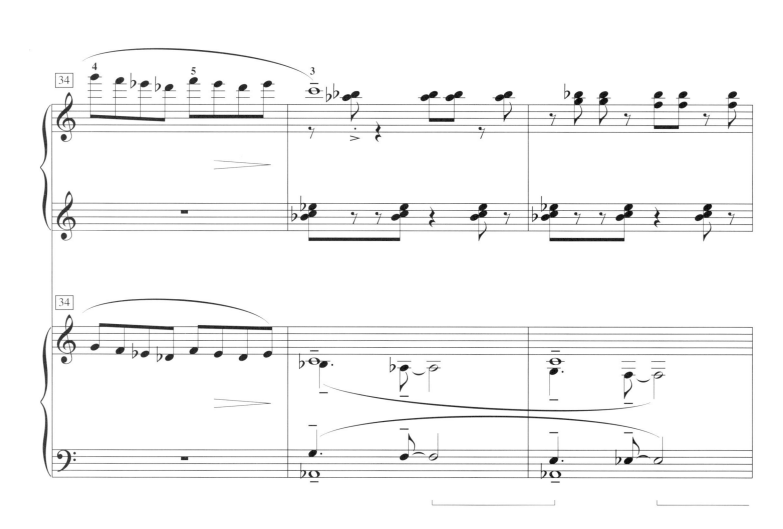

Crescent City Connection

By Eugénie R. Rocherolle

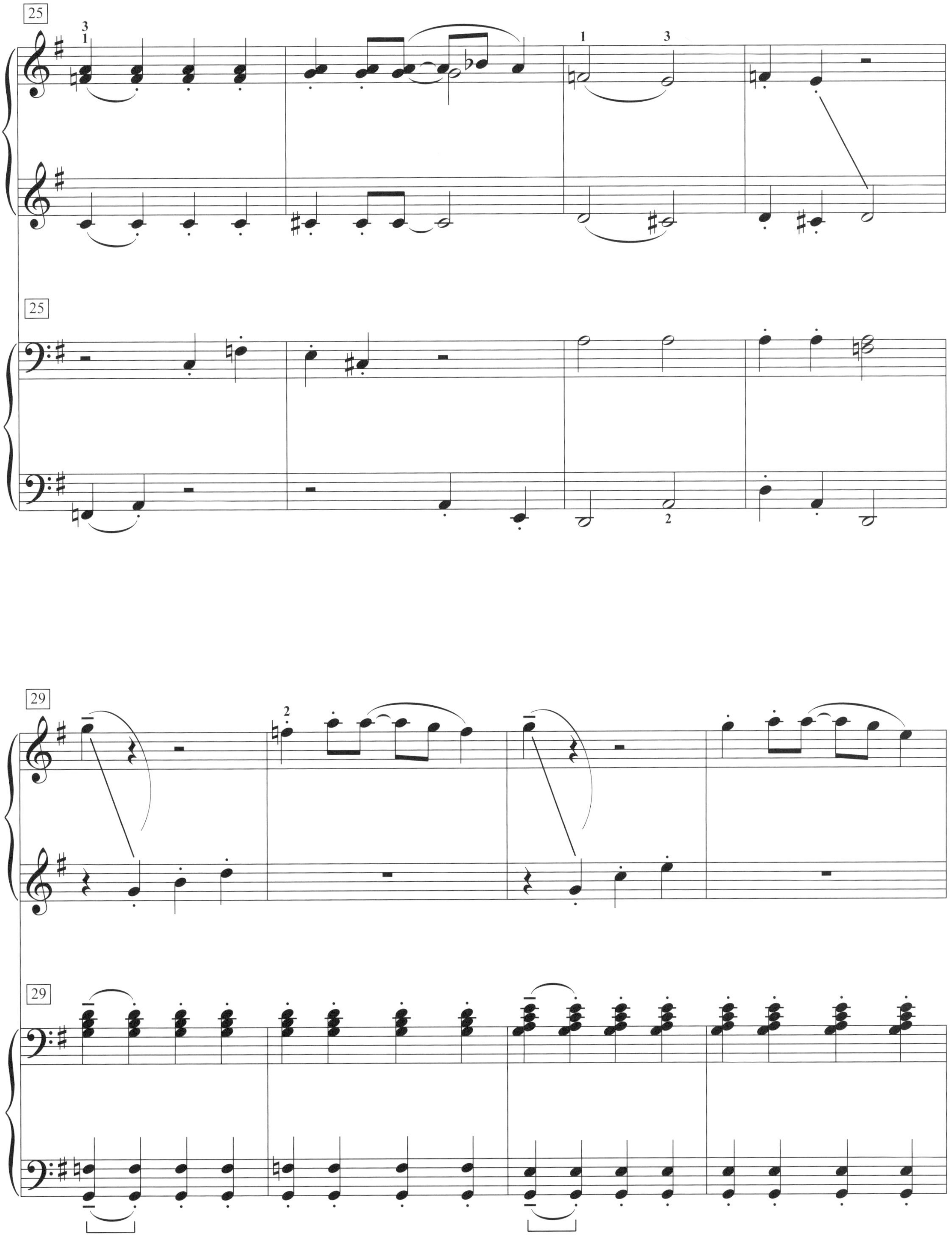
25
25
29
29

simile

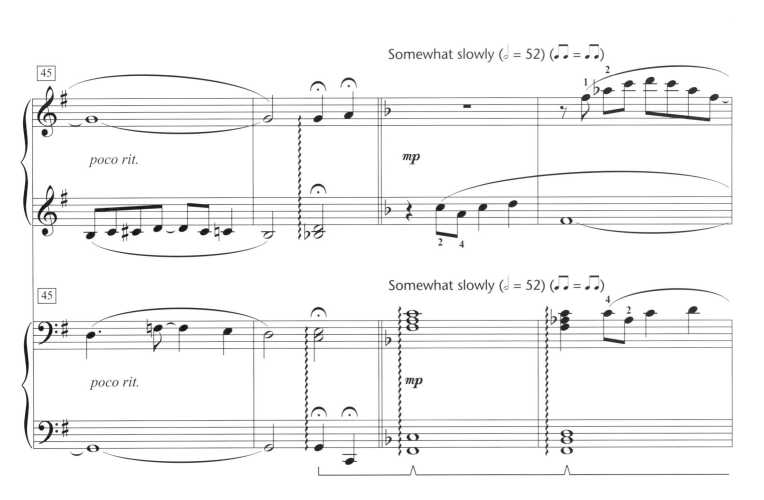

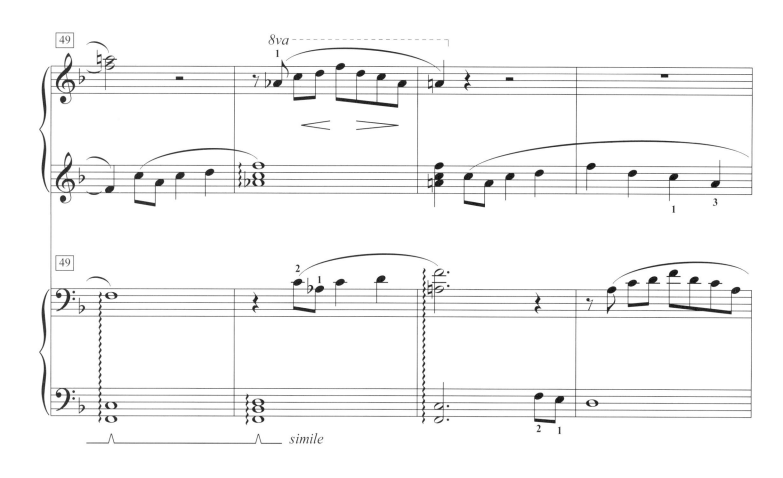

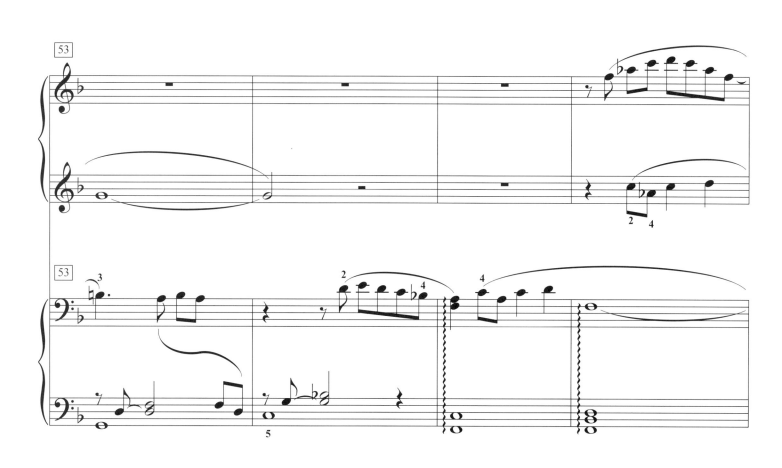

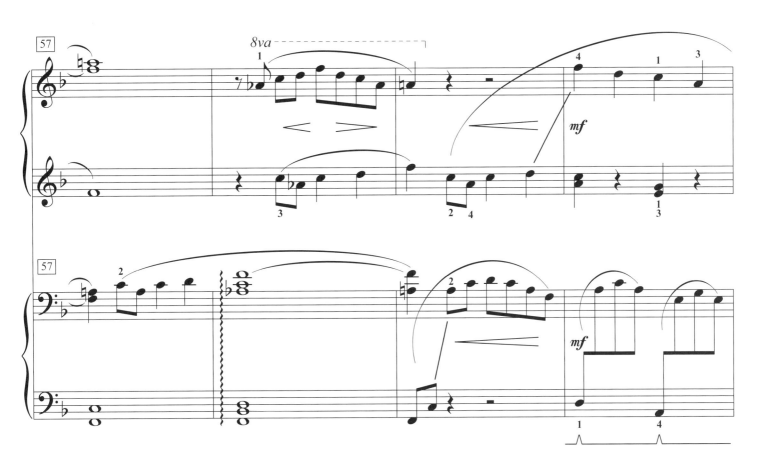

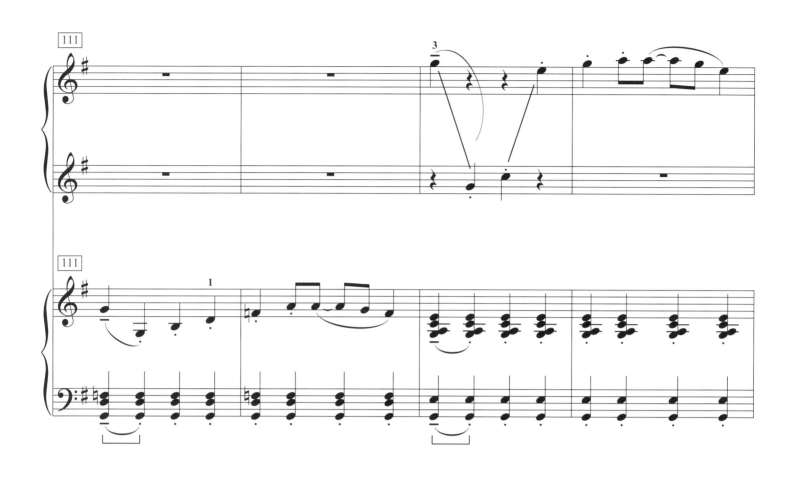

Prime Time

Commissioned by the Music Educators of Greater Annapolis

By Eugénie Rocherolle

36

A Wind of Promise

Commissioned by the Kansas Walnut Valley Music Teachers Association

By Wendy Stevens

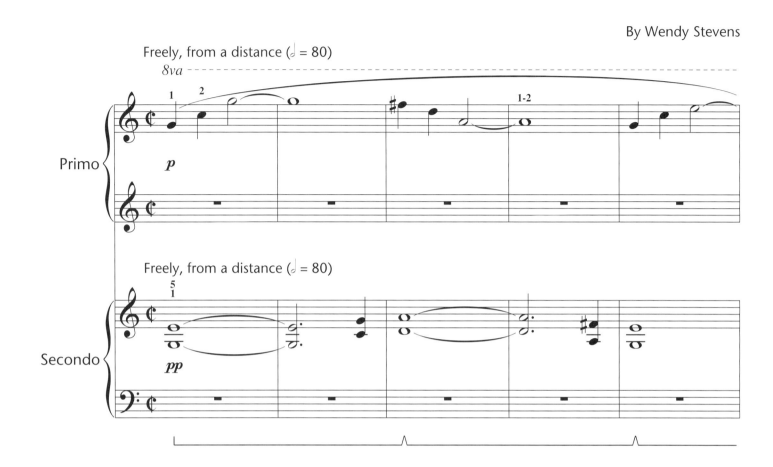

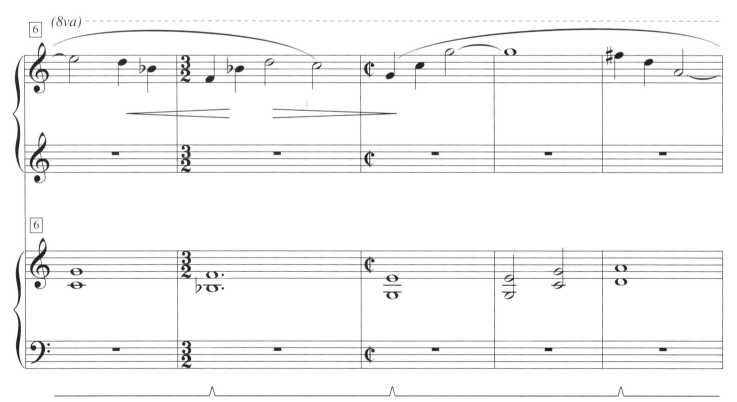

If performed with multiple pianos, the introduction may be played by one set of players stationed in the back (or side) for a special effect.
All players begin in m. 16.

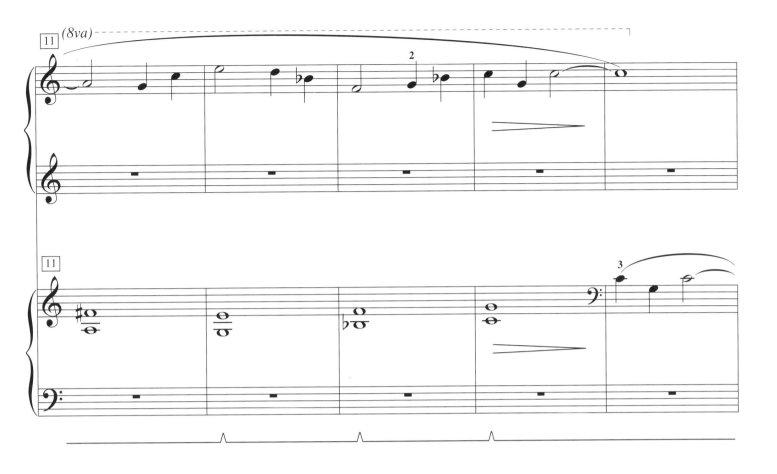

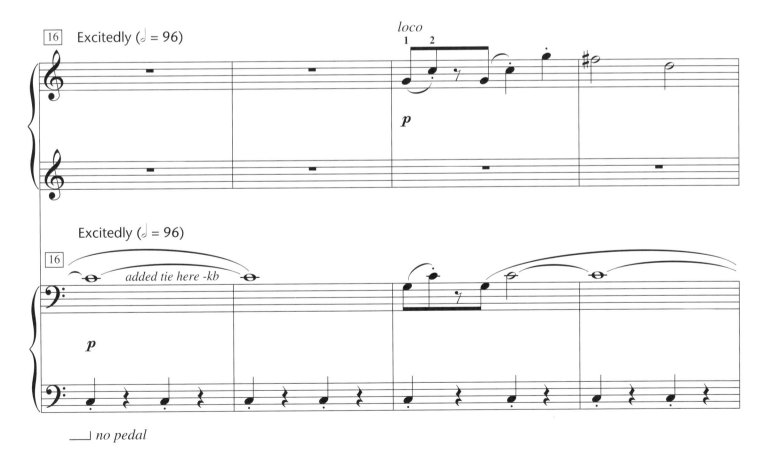

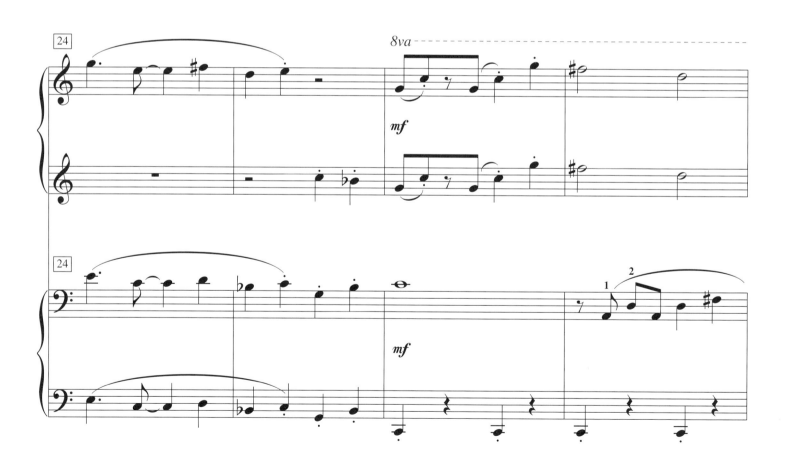

Calmly, like a gentle breeze

Calmly, like a gentle breeze

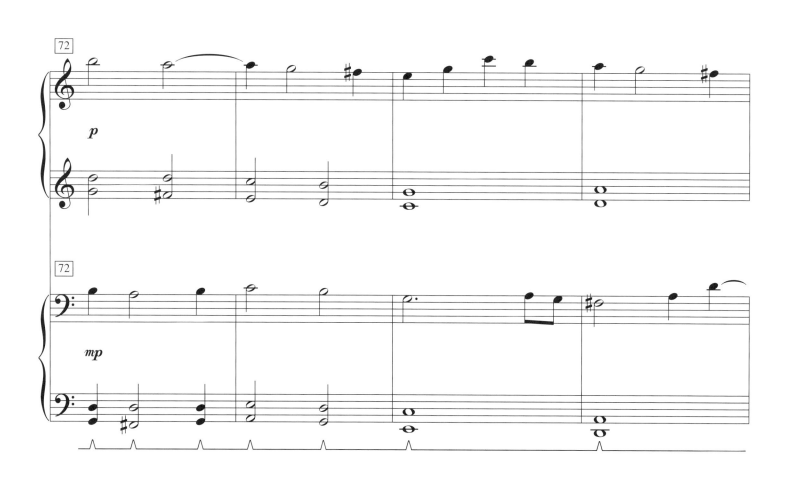

52

Commissioned by the 2004 Goshen College Piano Workshop and Academy

Yearning

By Phillip Keveren

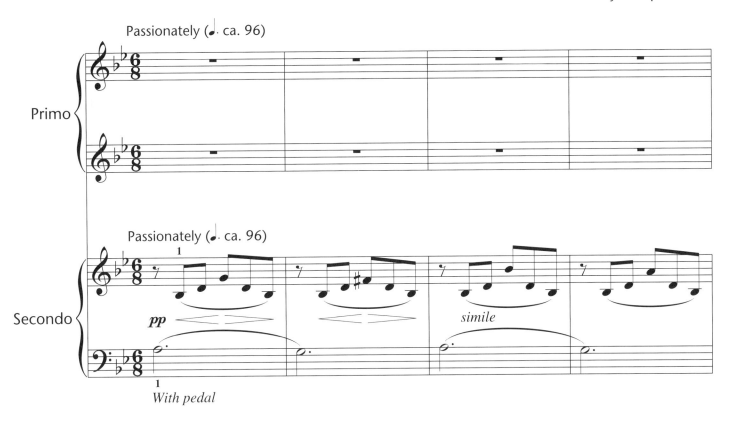

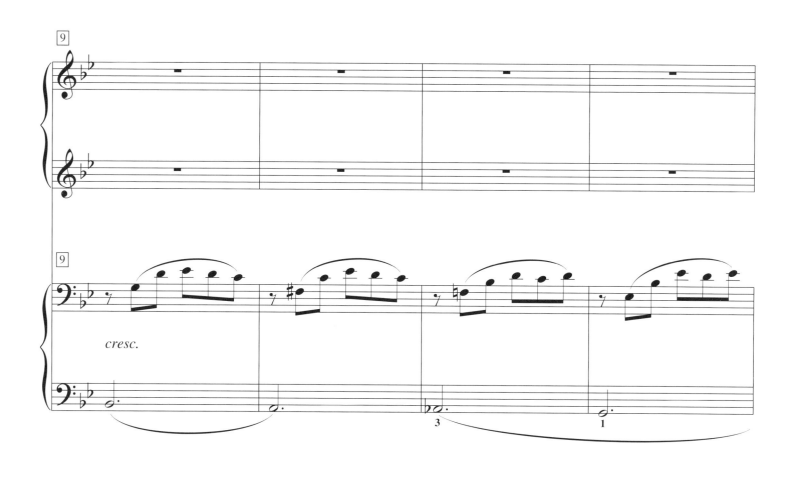

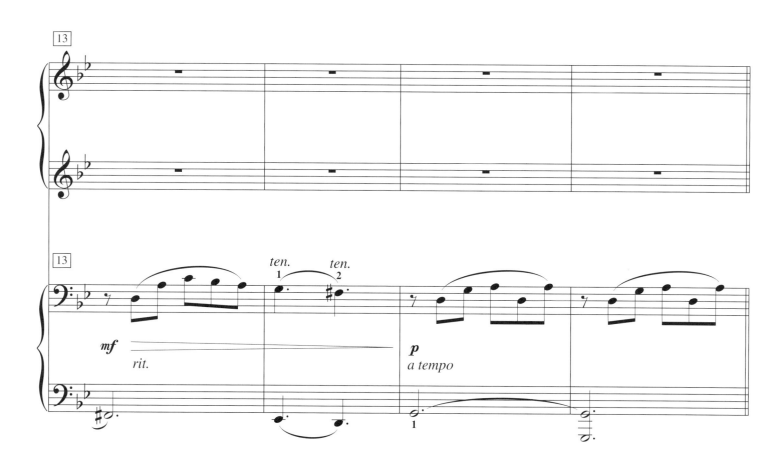

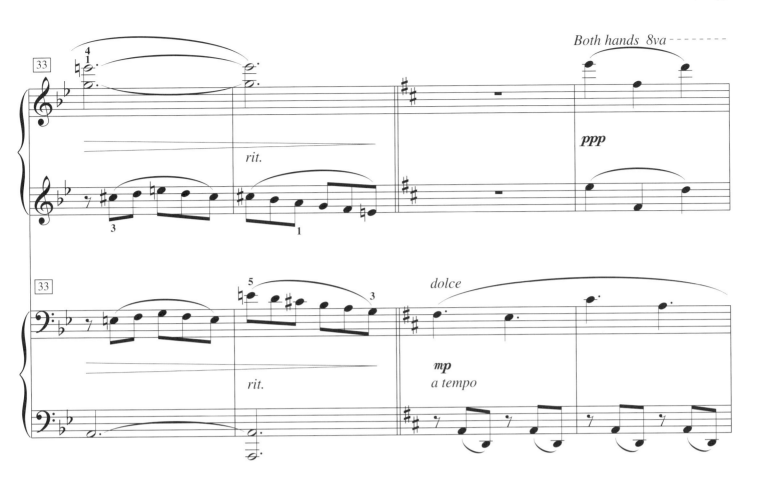

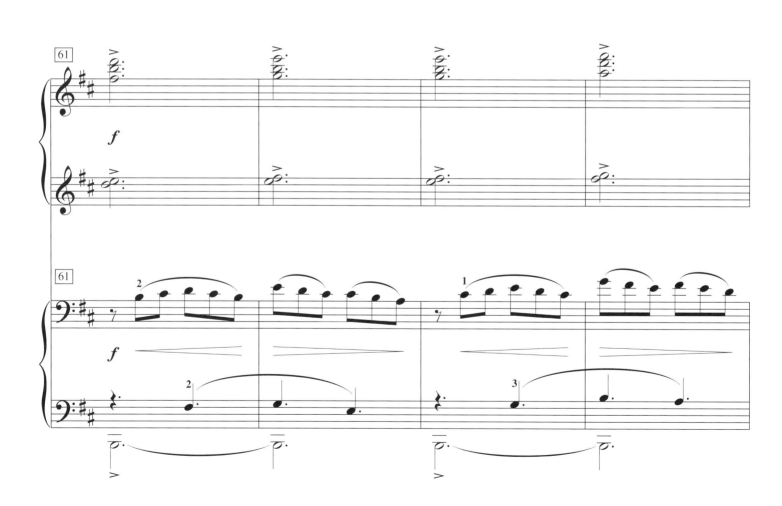

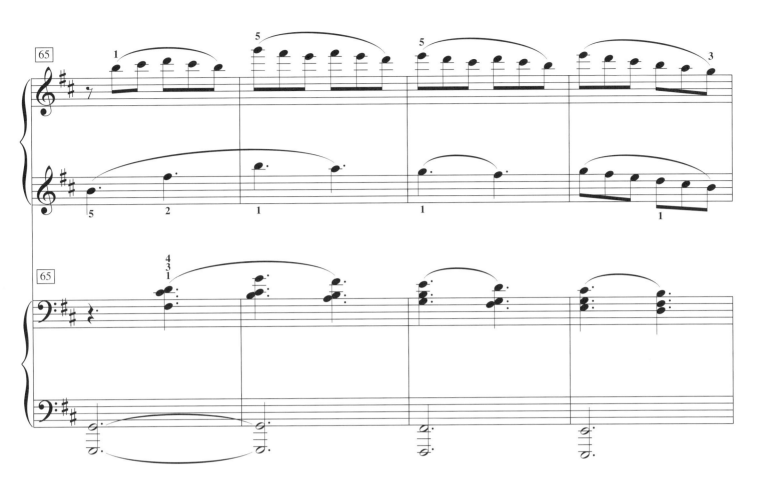

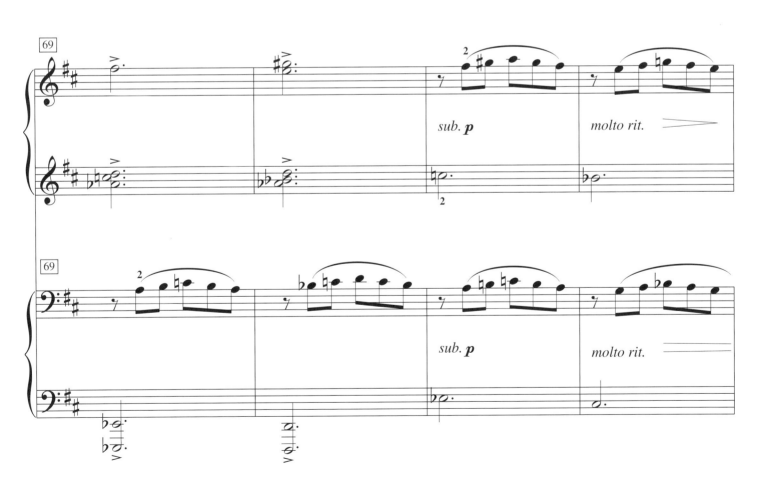

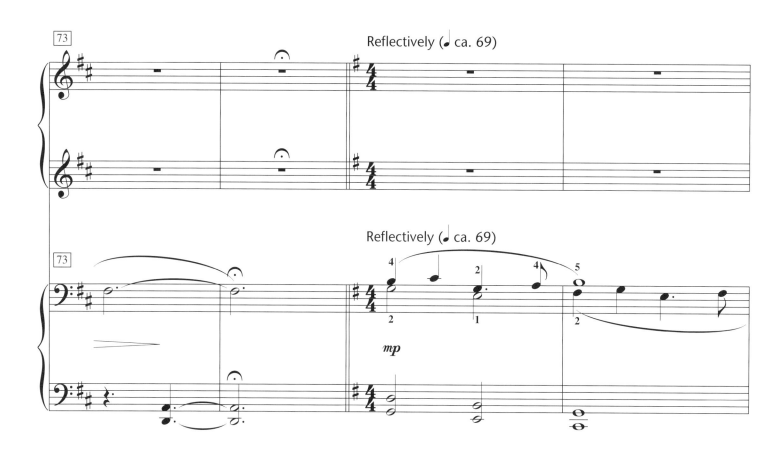

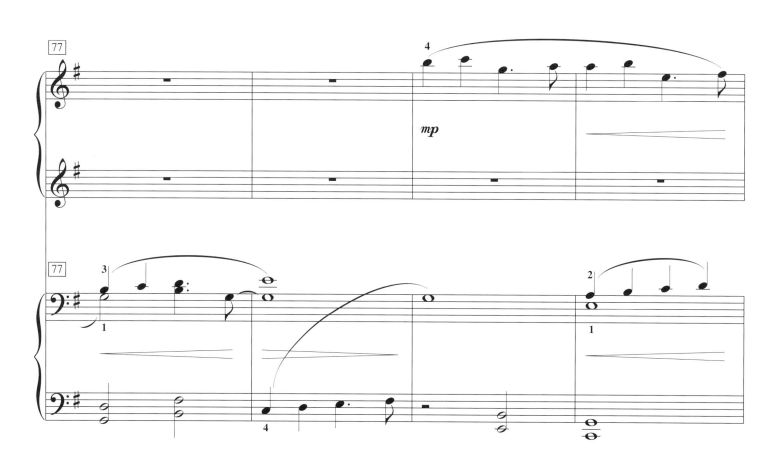

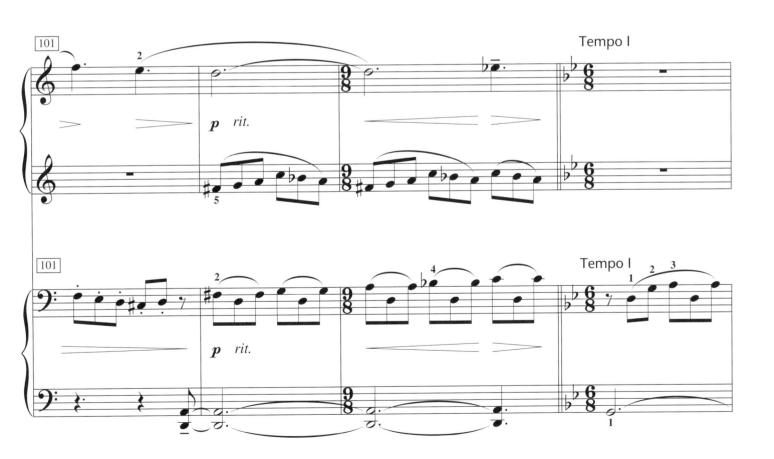

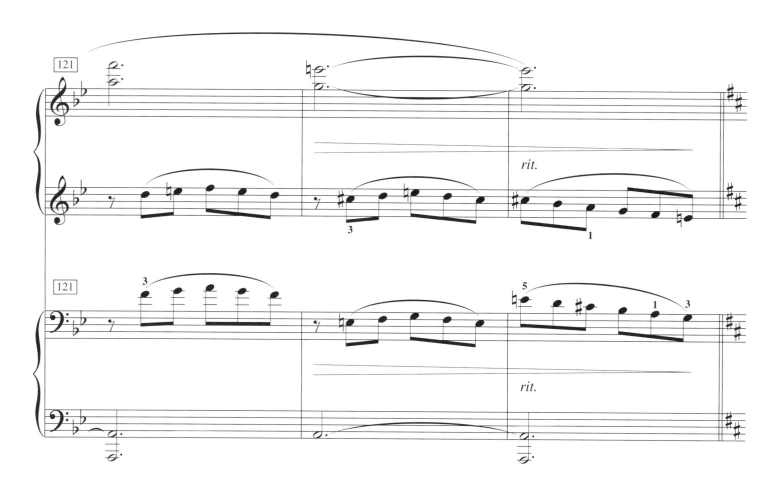

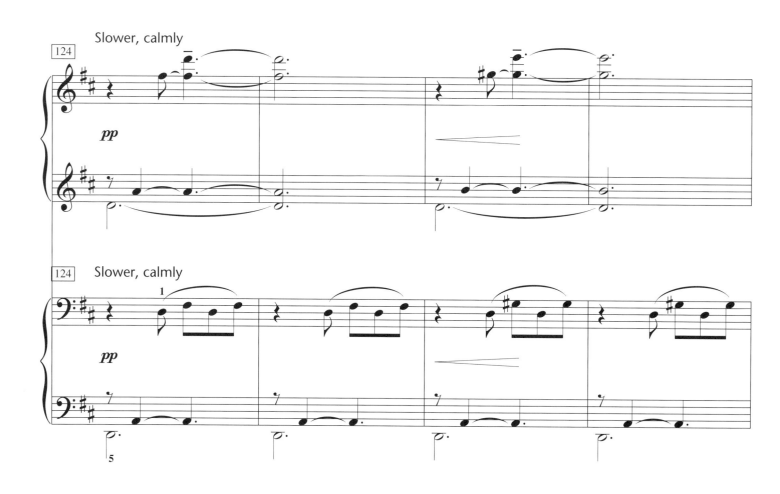

COMPOSER SHOWCASE
HAL LEONARD STUDENT PIANO LIBRARY

This series showcases great original piano music from our **Hal Leonard Student Piano Library** family of composers, including Bill Boyd, Phillip Keveren, Carol Klose, Jennifer Linn, Mona Rejino, Eugénie Rocherolle and more. Carefully graded for easy selection, each book contains gems that are certain to become tomorrow's classics!

BILL BOYD

JAZZ BITS (AND PIECES)
Early Intermediate Level
00290312 11 Solos.........................$6.99

JAZZ DELIGHTS
Intermediate Level
00240435 11 Solos.........................$7.99

JAZZ FEST
Intermediate Level
00240436 10 Solos.........................$7.99

JAZZ PRELIMS
Early Elementary Level
00290032 12 Solos.........................$6.99

JAZZ SKETCHES
Intermediate Level
00220001 8 Solos...........................$6.99

JAZZ STARTERS
Elementary Level
00290425 10 Solos.........................$6.99

JAZZ STARTERS II
Late Elementary Level
00290434 11 Solos.........................$7.99

JAZZ STARTERS III
Late Elementary Level
00290465 12 Solos.........................$7.99

THINK JAZZ!
Early Intermediate Level
00290417 Method Book...............$10.99

TONY CARAMIA

JAZZ MOODS
Intermediate Level
00296728 8 Solos...........................$6.95

SUITE DREAMS
Intermediate Level
00296775 4 Solos...........................$6.99

SONDRA CLARK

DAKOTA DAYS
Intermediate Level
00296521 5 Solos...........................$6.95

FAVORITE CAROLS FOR TWO
Intermediate Level
00296530 5 Duets..........................$7.99

FLORIDA FANTASY SUITE
Intermediate Level
00296766 3 Duets..........................$7.95

ISLAND DELIGHTS
Intermediate Level
00296666 4 Solos...........................$6.95

THREE ODD METERS
Intermediate Level
00296472 3 Duets..........................$6.95

MATTHEW EDWARDS

CONCERTO FOR YOUNG PIANISTS
FOR 2 PIANOS, FOUR HANDS
Intermediate Level Book/CD
00296356 3 Movements $16.95

CONCERTO NO. 2 IN G MAJOR
FOR 2 PIANOS, 4 HANDS
Intermediate Level Book/CD
00296670 3 Movements.................$16.95

PHILLIP KEVEREN

MOUSE ON A MIRROR
Late Elementary Level
00296361 5 Solos...........................$6.95

MUSICAL MOODS
Elementary/Late Elementary Level
00296714 7 Solos...........................$5.95

ROMP! – BOOK/CD PACK
A DIGITAL KEYBOARD ENSEMBLE FOR SIX PLAYERS
Intermediate Level
00296549 Book/CD........................$9.95
00296548 Book/GM Disk $9.95

SHIFTY-EYED BLUES
Late Elementary Level
00296374 5 Solos...........................$6.99

TEX-MEX REX
Late Elementary Level
00296353 6 Solos...........................$5.95

CAROL KLOSE

CORAL REEF SUITE
Late Elementary Level
00296354 7 Solos...........................$6.99

DESERT SUITE
Intermediate Level
00296667 6 Solos...........................$7.99

FANCIFUL WALTZES
Early Intermediate Level
00296473 5 Solos...........................$7.95

GARDEN TREASURES
Late Intermediate Level
00296787 5 Solos...........................$7.99

TRADITIONAL CAROLS FOR TWO
Late Elementary Level
00296557 5 Duets..........................$7.99

WATERCOLOR MINIATURES
Early Intermediate Level
00296848 7 Solos...........................$7.99

JENNIFER LINN

AMERICAN IMPRESSIONS
Intermediate Level
00296471 6 Solos...........................$7.99

CHRISTMAS IMPRESSIONS
Intermediate Level
00296706 8 Solos...........................$6.99

JUST PINK
Elementary Level
00296722 9 Solos...........................$6.99

LES PETITES IMAGES
Late Elementary Level
00296664 7 Solos...........................$7.99

LES PETITES IMPRESSIONS
Intermediate Level
00296355 6 Solos...........................$7.99

REFLECTIONS
Late Intermediate Level
00296843 5 Solos...........................$7.99

FOR MORE INFORMATION, SEE YOUR LOCAL MUSIC DEALER, OR WRITE TO:

HAL•LEONARD®
CORPORATION
7777 W. BLUEMOUND RD. P.O. BOX 13819 MILWAUKEE, WI 53213

For full descriptions and song lists for the books listed here, and to view a complete list of titles in this series, please visit our website at www.halleonard.com

TALES OF MYSTERY
Intermediate Level
00296769 6 Solos...........................$7.99

MONA REJINO

CIRCUS SUITE
Late Elementary Level
00296665 5 Solos...........................$5.95

JUST FOR KIDS
Elementary Level
00296840 8 Solos...........................$7.99

MERRY CHRISTMAS MEDLEYS
Intermediate Level
00296799 5 Solos...........................$7.99

PORTRAITS IN STYLE
Early Intermediate Level
00296507 6 Solos...........................$7.99

EUGÉNIE ROCHEROLLE

JAMBALAYA
FOR 2 PIANOS, 8 HANDS
Intermediate Level
00296654 Piano Ensemble............$9.99

JAMBALAYA
FOR 2 PIANOS, 4 HANDS
Intermediate Level
00296725 Piano Duo (2 Pianos) $7.95

TOUR FOR TWO
Late Elementary Level
00296832 6 Duets..........................$7.99

CHRISTOS TSITSAROS

DANCES FROM AROUND THE WORLD
Early Intermediate Level
00296688 7 Solos...........................$6.95

POETIC MOMENTS
Intermediate Level
00296403 8 Solos...........................$7.95

SONATINA HUMORESQUE
Late Intermediate Level
00296772 3 Movements $6.99

SONGS WITHOUT WORDS
Intermediate Level
00296506 9 Solos...........................$7.95

THROUGHOUT THE YEAR
Late Elementary Level
00296723 12 Duets........................$6.95

ADDITIONAL COLLECTIONS

AMERICAN PORTRAITS
by Wendy Stevens
Intermediate Level
00296817 6 Solos...........................$7.99

MONDAY'S CHILD
(A CHILD'S BLESSINGS)
by Deborah Brady
Intermediate Level
00296373 7 Solos...........................$6.95

PLAY THE BLUES!
by Luann Carman (Method Book)
Early Intermediate Level
00296357 10 Solos.........................$8.99

PUPPY DOG TALES
by Deborah Brady
Elementary Level
00296718 5 Solos...........................$6.95

WORLD GEMS
FOR 2 PIANOS, 8 HANDS
arr. by Amy O'Grady
Early Intermediate Level
00296505 6 Folk Songs $6.95